I0411316

Message to Congress
Nero Continues to
Fiddle as Rome Burns

by

Roy Eaton

Soldier Boy Publications

Copyright © 2013 Roy Eaton

All rights reserved.

ISBN-10: 1484916735
ISBN-13: 978-1484916735

ENDORSEMENTS

Eaton's *Message to Congress,* subtitled: *Nero Continues to Fiddle as Rome Burns,* is the perfect follow-up to his *Makers, Shakers and Takers.* In this latest work, he chides congress for their seeming inability or will to address the serious issues facing our country. Eaton not only identifies and clearly explains the issues, he also offers cogent potential resolutions to each. If every member of congress reads this thought provoking work, maybe, just maybe congress would once again regain the ability to govern.

— Joseph DiLalla
Author of *Bloodlines*
Naples, Florida

The first to inhabit our great nation, the Native Americans, lived according to the ideology of the "Seventh Generation." With everything they did, they were conscious of how it would effect seven generations beyond them. It seems that the United States of America needs to take a step back and realize whether or not it is allowing this tradition - that exists on the very same soil - to take any kind of precedence in its decision making procedures.

Through his book of relevant, insightful and ingenious ideas, Roy Eaton describes ways in which our country can once again, begin to think in the realm of long-term rather than right this minute.

The Native Americans had it right. After all, they survived what our ancestors did to them. So let's take stock in what they have to say, and let's all stop and read Roy Eaton's "Message to Congress: Nero Continues to Fiddle as Rome Burns." Both shine a beacon of light on the ever darkening days our country is continuing to face.

Congratulations to Roy for his vision, his passion and his latest publication.

— Natalie Strom
Coastal Breeze News
Marco Island, Florida

Roy Eaton offers practical, well considered, doable recommendations to address the grave economic and civic issues of our time. The author quotes Thomas Jefferson regarding one of our most pervasive problems. "It is incumbent on every generation to pay its own debt as it goes." He quotes Jefferson again in his summation of "MESSAGE TO CONGRESS-Nero Continues to Fiddle as Rome Burns." "The greatest good we can do our country is to heal party divisions and make them one people."

Readers should consider urging their representatives in Congress to engage in substantive discussions which will lead, finally, to bipartisan solutions to the pressing problems afflicting our country.

— Jane A. Marlowe
Coastal Breeze News
Marco Island, Florida

In my life I have never seen Congress so absolutely dysfunctional. And the most outrageous part of the current congressional inertia is the fact that it is a 100% self-inflicted wound brought about by one party's singular goal of making the President they loathe a complete failure. It is a fact that proposals from the political right have actually been voted down by their very sponsors as soon as it was learned that the President was willing to go along with the idea.

The suggestions contained within this book are not radical or require loss of any rights to enact. They are, frankly, chock full of the one thing Congress seems to lack these days: Common sense! You might not agree with every detail of every proposal, but for the parts you do agree on, the real challenge will be for you to contact your elected officials and tell them how you feel about the various issues they need to resolve. Then hold them accountable each November.

— Will Dresser
Author of 'Wes Franklin' International Thrillers
Las Vegas, NV

ALSO

BY

ROY EATON

Soldier Boy

The Chosen Few *

Makers, Shakers, and Takers

*(Co-Author Joe DiLalla)

DEDICATION

I dedicate this book to the veterans who have honorably served our country, to the families of our armed forces who have endured the agony of separation and loss, to our wounded warriors who honorably bear the scars of battle, and to the members of our armed forces who selflessly sacrificed their lives in combat to protect their 'fellow man' and to guarantee our nation's sovereignty and our democratic way of life.

ACKNOWLEDGMENTS

To those who contributed to making this publication possible.

To Will Dresser: thank you for editing my manuscript and for doing the layout and formatting for this book and its cover.

To Jane Marlowe and Natalie Strom: thank you for editing my work at Coastal Breeze News.

To Dave Wilson: thank you for the technical support and for assisting in formatting.

To Joe DiLalla: thank you for your invaluable input and for reviewing and editing my work.

To Publisher Val Simon of the Coastal Breeze News: thank you for granting permission to publish my imaged articles and the newsprint contained in this publication and for the assistance your staff provided in editing my work.

To my wife Debra: thank you for reviewing my manuscript, and for providing the opportunity and inspiration to complete this work.

CONTENTS

PREFACE

Time has come to address the concerns and interests of all Americans.

Humorist and author Dr. Jim Boren once said, "Taxation *with* representation ain't so hot either." Your behavior has done much to support this assessment, but your reign of indecisiveness, disagreement, and gridlock is about to end. On November 6, the American people voted to retain our present administration and split Congress. Therefore, it is time you come to grips with the inevitable conclusion that you must succumb to compromise. In case you are not familiar with the term, it is defined as: "a settlement of a dispute between two or more sides, which agree to accept less than they originally wanted." If you manage to succeed in the art of compromise, you may discover that you expand your credentials to include the singular title of 'statesman.'

For those of your number who are unfamiliar with this term, it is defined as: "a 'man' who is widely respected for integrity and impartial concern for the public good." What a noble concept. Perhaps if you decide to emulate the selflessness of our forefathers and follow in their footsteps, which enabled our country to become the greatest nation that ever existed on our planet, you will dramatically raise your current, miserable 13 percent approval rating. You may restore the respect, trust, and admiration of the constituents who elected you and a nation which has depended on your once honorable institution for governance.

To clear up any misconception about the purpose of this book, I will tell you, first and foremost, I am neither a Democrat nor Republican. I am an American. My political affiliation is Independent. Therefore my views are not directed toward any one party, but rather to an inept, wavering Congress that has lost sight of its purpose and whom it is they truly represent. This Congress has failed to heed the wisdom of former President Rutherford B. Hayes, who believed that "one serves his party best by serving his country best." For too long, Congress has deluded itself and the American people that gridlock is the instrument of choice to maintain a steady course. This may have appeared to work during prosperous times, but in reality, failed to address the underlying problems that smoldered under a smokescreen of nominal success.

Our election process chose you to join or rejoin the legislative branch entrusted to enact the laws that govern our nation. You must understand when you took the oath of office, that you assumed an awesome duty to all Americans, not just the members of your respective parties. The selections made on November 6 will prove inconsequential if, once again, you fail to compromise and address the urgent issues at hand. The time has come for all members of both chambers of this once honorable institution to become more centrist.

I realize some of you believe that the Senate or House in which you presently reside, will never reach agreement on critical areas such as Social Security, Medicare, immigration, and tax reforms. However, you have no choice but to do so even though you may have to make concessions and consent to majority rule. We, as a nation, have serious concerns that need to be addressed and numerous programs that are in dire need of restructuring; modifications that must be fair, rational, and constructive. No problem is insurmountable if you are open to suggestion and compromise. Although your resolutions may differ, there is common ground: the well-being of our country and the public you were elected to serve. And, if there are members of the Senate who choose to consistently invoke the filibuster to prevent legislation from being enacted that represents the will of the majority, then their constituents should give serious consideration to immediately recalling these recalcitrant obstructionists from the upper chamber.

What I fail to understand is how some of you have justified your willingness to compromise your integrity and oath of office by catering to special interests, yet have been unwilling to compromise to serve the best interests of the country you were elected to serve.

I believe our government should champion fiscal restraint, for you must collectively ensure that our nation remains secure and unchallenged, that our economy once again becomes robust, and that our nation's sovereignty is never in question. I also believe you should display empathy toward our fellow man, for you have a moral obligation to help the sick, poor, and elderly Americans who are truly incapable of helping themselves.

If you continue to lack the sense and tenacity to solve our country's problems and wish to delegate the responsibility to others, instead of appointing fact-finding committees, perhaps you should appoint a bi-partisan **fact-facing** committee to address the issues. Unlike the Simpson-Bowles Commission, gather a board of voters who have never held public office, have no political aspirations, have a balanced economic agenda, are not obligated to a specific party or special interest group, and are proportionately representative of the general population. Let them brainstorm for a day or two. I'm sure they'll provide an ample supply of innovative ideas for you to consider. Perhaps you ought to visit our libraries, gyms and grocery stores, and our malls, barber shops, and town halls, not to campaign, but to listen. Your constituents most likely have more common sense than many of your peers, and far more valuable and practical advice to offer than you will hear from your colleagues in future committee discussions.

Unfortunately, most of my friends and acquaintances are correct when they say no one wants to listen. There once was a time when the average American could speak candidly to his or her representative and provide sound ideas that were actually considered. It seems in today's world unless one is a corporate CEO, a lobbyist, celebrated athlete, fellow politician, actor, media star, or billionaire, our representatives believe we have little to contribute to the intellectual hierarchy that occupies the great hall in which you legislate. Sadly, many of you are detached from your constituents, and when you do address the voter, you often seek admiration and approval rather than honest assessment, often admonishing those who wish to express an alternative view. This disdainful attitude is spreading through our society, for we have become a polarized nation where neither side wishes to consider the other's conflicting views.

You have grave concerns that need to be addressed, including the immediate removal of government personnel from host countries which fail to protect diplomats from insurgent and terrorist activity, and the immediate withdrawal of military personnel from combative arenas that expose troops to intentional friendly fire. As to the numerous programs in dire need of structural reform, I urge you as an **American voter** to work on our behalf to make program modifications which are fair, rational, and constructive. Although your revisions will have to be substantial, most reforms should be graduated in order to safeguard program recipients and bring about effective change which will not shock our fragile economy.

The future of our great nation will be decided by the actions of our newly elected 113th Congress. However, you have little time to continue to bathe in victory for time is not running out, it has run out. We recently avoided going over an immediate fiscal cliff. But that was addressable and miniscule when compared to the pending economic calamity that our nation faces if you fail to recognize, confront, and address the numerous problems that have been ignored by your predecessors, including our massive annual deficits and spiraling debt. If you, our American Congress, fail to implement structural changes that will eliminate deficits and reduce our massive debt, America will soon become a fragment of its former greatness, another footnote to a history of former great civilizations which succumbed to indecisiveness, disagreement, gridlock, and discontent, preceded by greed, arrogance, complacency, and inattentiveness.

Former President Bill Clinton said, "There is nothing wrong in America that can't be fixed with what is right in America." Former President George Bush said, "We are not limited by what we have done, or what we have left undone. We are limited only by what we are willing to do." I ask you to think of all that is right in America, and reconsider what you are willing to do to fix what is wrong.
Your actions will determine if our nation becomes a mere historical annotation in the centuries to come, or a nation that continues to inspire and aspire. I pray it is the latter.

INTRODUCTION

Roman Emperor Nero, during his reign, occupied himself with unimportant matters while neglecting priorities during pending crises, much like our 112th Congress which spent most of its time preoccupied with bickering and posturing with their counterparts and contemplating what a woman should be allowed to do with her body while avoiding passage of legislation that would guarantee a woman's constitutional right to equal pay for equal work. Congress grudgingly avoided the 'fiscal cliff,' but failed to address the major issues that confront our great, but struggling nation. Only when forced to vote last-minute legislation did they do so with reservation and minimal co-operation. The result was an incomprehensive legislative package that provided permanent tax relief to 98 percent of tax paying Americans without providing a means to pay for the additional increases to our annual budget and massive spiraling debt. Most importantly, it failed to address the major programs that are in dire need of modification which include income tax, Social Security, Medicare, and immigration. Nor did it address alterations that need to be made to Medicaid and to our new universal healthcare program and taxpayer-funded government pensions and benefits.

There is no question that the "fiscal cliff" compromise was a step in the right direction for it avoided a catastrophe. During this stage of our frail economic recovery, there is little doubt that our current rate of taxation for most Americans had to be retained, that unemployment benefits needed to be extended, and that taxes on capital gains needed to be raised for the top two percent. And, considering the middle class will most likely be expected to bear additional future hardships, it is fair to expect the wealthiest in our society to contribute a little more of their incomes.

What is not just is the unreasonably low five million dollar inheritance tax limitation and the permanency of the continuance of the Bush tax cuts for the remaining 98 percent of taxpayers. Many economists believe funding for the latter continuance unsustainable and the tax reduction should not have been made permanent, but instead, should have been linked to GNP and phased back to the Clinton tax rate once the economy has fully recovered. The inheritance tax threshold, one of the most unfair forms of taxation, should have been set at a much higher level. I realize that many of the wealthiest Americans have used every tax shelter available to accumulate wealth, which further illustrates the need to reform our current tax structure. But, this should not prevent the raising of the limitation of a tax that penalizes wealth accumulation when earned and again upon death.

As for continued discontent among our representatives, compromise rarely satisfies both parties. Our governing forefathers designed our current system of government to function in a manner that would ultimately result in concessions to majority rule. The events leading up to our fiscal cliff calamity illustrates that Congress has ignored this form of statesmanship and opted instead, to play a very contentious chess game with the highest of stakes wagered, the sovereignty of our great nation. A game too often played by career politicians whose every move is cunningly predetermined by special interests overseers who benefit from their participation.

The next major obstacle that faces our administration and Congress is the raising of the debt ceiling. I would like to think that Congress has gotten the message and will work diligently to arrive at a consensus that will allow the ceiling to be raised without frightening and destabilizing our markets and disappointing nations that look to America for stability and guidance; an agreement that broadly addresses our spiraling deficits and massive debt in a comprehensive, progressive, and fair manner. However, currently, there is no indication this can be achieved within a two month time period. Although I believe we should not continue to kick reforms down the road, for this mortgaging of the future poses an equally serious risk to our credit rating, our standard of living, and our nation's sovereignty, I do not believe we should hold the debt ceiling hostage, for this, too, poses serious consequences.

If the President resubmits a balanced approach which introduces spending cuts that are fair, progressive, and non-punitive to any one sector, I believe Congress should work to implement these reforms. If our President fails to meet these expectations, Congress has the responsibility and ability to introduce and pass legislation that will address these concerns. This is why our constitution created three distinct branches to balance power.

If our senators and congressmen disregard party lines and decide to talk with one another rather than at one another and seriously take time to collectively and rationally consider solutions to our fiscal crises, the path will be difficult, but not impossible to navigate.

Should our representatives fail to address and collectively work to correct the problems that confront our great nation, we should consider replacing every member of Congress when their term is up. This would send a clear message to our representatives that we hold them individually and collectively accountable for providing legislation that will defend our country, strengthen our economy, and guarantee our sovereignty. It will unequivocally convey that continued confrontation and failure are no longer acceptable and that 'we the people' expect our representatives to honorably discharge the duties of their office. In the future, we should never again vote for a politician who has pledged a commitment to any one person or entity. Such pledges, should at best, be considered disloyal, and at worst, treasonous which is defined as 'a violation of the allegiance owed by somebody to his or her country.' Voters have the indisputable power to periodically remind our representatives their commitment is to our country and not to individuals, to special interests groups, or to self-serving agendas. Such a voter response would certainly indirectly impose term limitations, a restriction that will never be passed by self-serving politicians who fail to understand their tenure is temporary and not a career entitlement.

Regardless of party affiliation, all Americans should encourage our President and Congress to reconcile differences and collectively choose the correct path to prosperity. Should they fail; every generation will bear the unimaginable consequences.

CHAPTER ONE

TAX REFORM

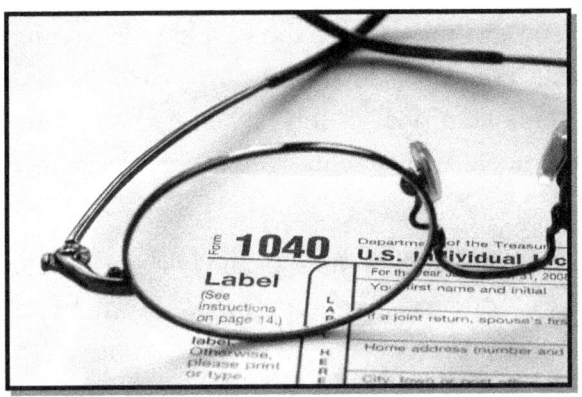

It is correct to criticize Congress for past failures, because their lack of insight, complacency, inattentiveness, and inability to compromise has led to our current fiscal dilemma. Congress's incompetence and laissez faire attitude has compromised the integrity of a balanced system of government that has nearly ceased to function. Two unfunded wars and an unfunded tax cut further exacerbated the need to raise taxes and substantially reduce spending to eliminate deficits and reduce long term indebtedness that can no longer be solely addressed by economic growth. The need for sizeable increases in revenues could force a complete overhaul of our current progressive system of taxation, while the need to considerably reduce costs could result in severe modifications to Social Security, Medicare, and Medicaid. If the trustee overseers of Social Security and Medicare had done their job to protect these fiscally endangered programs, there would be little need to address these 'entitlements' that have safeguarded those who have earned and paid for this umbrella of protection. Although these programs are technically 'entitlements' by definition, because our government gave each working American and our employers the 'right' to contribute current earnings to provide a safety net during the latter years of life, they are not an award, gift, or privilege, and should never be treated or referred to as such.

I do not profess to be an expert in reform, and the alternatives I am about to suggest may not be the best choices available. However, they represent concepts derived from a few hours of reflection, which represents a snippet in time when compared to the thousands of hours our elected representatives were given to consider these matters.

First, President Obama and Congress must determine if they want to modify our existing progressive form of taxation, which most Democrats prefer, convert to a flat tax which many Republicans seem to favor, or implement a European-type value-added sales tax that unfairly taxes those who earn the least and spend the most on the necessities of life.

Our current tax code is overly complicated and cumbersome, and fosters "irrational individual behavior and corporate avoidance." If our representatives decide our existing code is the fairest and best income generating form of taxation, then unfair and irrational loopholes that solely favor the rich and special interests must be abolished. No longer can we subsidize successful corporations like Exxon that reap massive profits, yet seek tax payer incentives. No longer should hedge funds be allowed to benefit from having their profits taxed as capital gains rather than at the appropriate tax rate. Nor can we allow profits from vulture capitalism to be intentionally undervalued and taxed at a deferred time. We cannot levy an unreasonably low threshold estate tax of $5 million on estates that exhaust accumulated wealth by again taxing the most successful workers and entrepreneurs at their passing. The capital gains tax should be tiered so that individuals with incomes under $400,000 investing in risky start-up companies that actually create jobs will be taxed more favorably than those who invest in the stock of proven companies which do little to create new positions. There should be a standard deduction of $25,000 per household, adjusted annually for inflation.

Should a flat tax be considered the fairest and selected path for generating revenue, then to be a truly just form of taxation, it should contain only one standard deduction for taxpayers with no special rate for capital gains. Currently, our tax system rewards those who have children, mortgages, are married, have subsidized health plans, and invest in IRA's or 401K's, while ignoring those who have either voluntarily or involuntarily selected a different path that does not qualify them for some or all of the above deductions.

All Americans should be treated equally under a non-progressive system. The standard deduction should include the current average standard interest deduction of $10,640, the present exemption for the average number of dependents per household of $9,880, the average grocery bill for a family of $6,443, the average cost to maintain a car of $8,003, the average contribution to IRA's or 401K's of $4,950, and the average health insurance coverage of $10,030 (average of $4,316 employee contribution to employer plans and $15,745 per family to a non-employer plan). The total standard deduction for all American households would be approximately $50,000 and should be adjusted annually to compensate for inflation. Anything over this dollar amount would be taxed at a flat rate to be determined. This manner of calculating the common deduction would be simple and fair, and provide most taxpayers with an opportunity to maintain a decent standard of living and a way to accumulate wealth.

I support either of the above tax structures if the former is modified, or the latter constructed as mentioned, but avidly oppose a European-style sales tax code that penalizes goods and services at every stage of production, and dramatically impacts the least affluent. Regardless of which format is chosen, a five percent millionaire surtax should be levied on incomes exceeding $5 million and a ten percent millionaire surtax on incomes exceeding $10 million until our national debt has been eliminated.

Henry Ford had the sense to ensure that his workers had the ability to purchase his own product. If American workers do not have the income to purchase the products and services they produce and provide, then demand will not meet supply and deflation will continue to dampen expansion.

The tax structure for business must be revamped as well. Tort and patent reforms must be implemented to prevent frivolous claims. Incentives must be introduced to discourage businesses from going abroad.

Small businesses must be granted easier access to credit. Variances should be issued to small start-up companies to by-pass trivial, duplicate, or irrational regulation. Universal health care must be streamlined to reduce the costs to small businesses which provide employee or personal coverage. One time tax amnesty tax credits should be granted to induce trillions of expatriated dollars sitting in foreign banks or invested in enterprises abroad to be returned to our economy, if invested in infrastructure, job training, equipment, and plant expansion, and equated to the number of jobs created. No major tax reform should be legislated unless linked to a balanced budget.

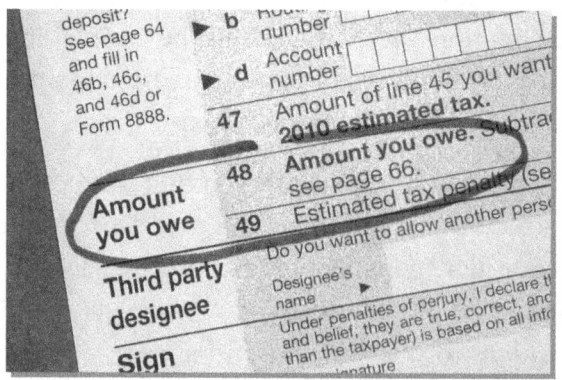

Contained in the 'fiscal cliff' compromise were certain additional options pertaining to the rollover of 401K's into Roth I.R.A's. This was primarily done to raise current revenues. But, to the best of my knowledge, these additions failed to adequately meet the needs of those approaching or already in retirement.

During our current economic downturn, a good number of aging Americans who normally reduce exposure to stocks by investing in fixed assets, sought to maximize gains by investing in riskier securities. Unlike some members of Congress who may have profited from their exemption from the regulations of insider trading, these seniors lost a substantial portion of their life savings. Other seniors opted to leave their funds in fixed instruments that created little additional wealth due to record low interest rates. Sadly, most of these investors have little or no time to recover losses or raise asset values, because regulations require partial withdrawal of proceeds starting at age 70.5. Therefore, Congress should either extend the mandatory beginning withdrawal age for I.R.A's and 401K's to correlate to the number of years that transpire during our current downturn, or permanently extend the initial extraction age to compensate for the increase in life expectancy. This is precisely what many in Congress seek to do with social security income distribution. For taxpayers with incomes under $250,000, Congress should extend the period in which to convert to Roth IRA's to three years, and consider treating this accumulation as a long term gain to increase conversion activity, compensate for losses incurred and increase current revenues.

CHAPTER TWO

SOCIAL SECURITY REFORM

I cannot, in good conscience, suggest modifications to Social Security without first addressing the reform recommendations announced by one of the most prestigious groups of influential business men in America, The Business Roundtable. The Business Roundtable, which consists of CEOs of the largest corporations in the United States, and represents roughly 33 percent of the total value of all U.S. stocks, recommended last week that the current age for Social Security and Medicare be extended to 70 for Americans currently under age 55.

It is ironic and disgraceful that several of the CEOs of companies that received generous taxpayer subsidies or bail-out assistance during our economic downturn, which several of them helped to create, are members of a roundtable that recommends delaying payments of benefits to which taxpayers are entitled.

Big businesses often refute big government for the establishment of social programs that benefit the public and are funded with taxpayer money. However, when their survival is threatened, these same companies believe in social corporate welfare. Business and worker well-being are interdependent, for the economic health of one is contingent upon the other. They are not synonymous though, for the value we place on life and the welfare of our society and country should far exceed the worth placed on the corporate sector.

I would like to think the roundtable's recommendation simply lacks insight, but I believe this is merely another illustration of corporate greed and indifference. It demonstrates callousness toward the American worker and the plight of the less fortunate; one more instance where the wealthiest among us often have the least compassion for their fellow man; one more example of big business's embracing of Darwin's theory of "survival of the fittest."

The Business Roundtable's recommendation should not be surprising, for most corporations have stopped funding company pension plans, have reduced or eliminated matching 401K contributions as well as contributions for employee health insurance. There is no doubt that our nation's CEOs are bright and resourceful. However, their endorsement expresses little sympathy for the less fortunate and illustrates their collective lack of understanding of the economic hardships most breadwinners of middle age families currently endure. Perhaps they would think differently if they lost their obscene salaries, often inflated fifty to a thousand times that of the average worker, and lost their 'golden parachutes,' either of which eliminates their need for any form of social safety net.

One must begin to question whether the welfare of the corporation has become far more important than the welfare of our nation and its people. I realize that business provides jobs that enable families to acquire the necessities and luxuries to sustain and enjoy life. But workers provide a valuable service and should be treated with dignity and respect and not regarded as disposable objects that can be replaced easily, even during a time when there are far more workers than available jobs.

It is unjust for CEOs to make recommendations that affect the distribution of income and benefits earned decades before many of their companies were formed. It is also unfair that credence be given to any proposal coming from any sector within the economy that is governed solely by its bottom line.

There is no doubt that our nation's indebtedness threatens our dollar and the sovereignty of our great nation, and that decades of complacency, unfettered capitalism, and government incompetence have made long term funding of our pledged entitlements unsustainable. However, unlike the roundtable's recommendation, solutions for reform must be fair, comprehensive, and implemented over an extended period of time, an approach that the corporate sector dislikes and neither party in Congress seems willing to address. No one generation should be required to immediately bear the entire burden of restructuring, especially one that has contributed over a prolonged period of time and has the least number of years to recover from reform. If we were to follow the roundtable's proposal, a 55 year old worker with 10 years of service can retire with full benefits at age 67, while a person at age 54 with 35 years of service, would have to wait another three years to retire at age 70. Also, it is immoral to unfairly penalize those approaching their mid-fifties, who face age discrimination seeking work, and are sandwiched between helping their children and assisting their aging parents.

It is estimated in its present form, the Social Security Trust can fully fund withdrawals until the year 2036, after which it will be able to fund only 75 percent of guaranteed incomes. To cut costs and build reserves that will protect the integrity of the Social Security Trust, I am recommending several incremental changes to Social Security that will address both the revenue and expense sides of the economic equation.

I realize that Social Security is not a personal investment account, although it could have originally been set up in such a manner with funds being automatically invested in government securities. Instead, the trust was devised to provide a safety net for retirees, their spouses and children, and the disabled. It is a sound program with nearly 99 percent of revenues being paid out in benefits. Although our indebtedness may force program reform, it is not Social Security that is bankrupting the system. **It is the system that is bankrupting Social Security.**

There is a misconception that funding for this program is insufficient due to the increase in the life expectancy of the worker and because retirees outnumber contributing workers. This is not the case when applied to the working spouse, for if one were to calculate the average worker and employer contributions for a current 66 year old from age 21 over a 45 year work-span, invested in government bonds and treasuries, the principal would, most likely, far exceed a million dollars. Even at a payout at today's historically low 30 year bond interest rate of approximately 3 percent, the annual amount paid to a recipient would exceed $30,000 a year without touching or annualizing the principal. However, the stay-at-home-spouse is another matter.

Some economists say current funding is insufficient, because stay-at-home spouses, who have not paid directly into the program, are dramatically diminishing the funds by receiving retirement income based on their working spouse's earnings. I fully understand the importance of having a stay-at-home parent during the most impressionable years of childhood. But, under current regulation, a stay-at-home spouse could theoretically collect a greater retirement income under their working spouse than a person who worked a lifetime with a far lower income.

Current regulations require that a worker complete 40 quarters of work (10 years) to be eligible to receive retirement income under his or her own merit. I do not believe it is unreasonable to ask both family members to qualify under their own work history. If either spouse chooses not to accumulate the required 40 quarters, then the working spouse should have the option of paying an additional payroll tax of 50 percent (not matched by employer) for each missing quarter needed to qualify for spouse eligibility. This would affect all Americans under the age of 35 who have not accumulated 40 quarters of credit.

A good number of Americans who believe in a progressive income tax code also believe in expanding the payroll tax limitation, because they believe the current tax is too regressive for it favors the wealthier taxpayers who do not have to contribute after they have reached the current threshold of $113,700. If the majority of Americans believe their contributions entitle them to an amount commensurate with what they and their employers have contributed, then an argument could be made that such an increase should proportionally raise the income amount to which the wealthiest are entitled. To avoid any implication of a double standard, I would continue to increase the current limit, but would tie it to the inflation rate, and proportionally base future earnings on contributions. Because of the indecent and unsustainable growing disparity between the ultra rich and remaining population and the extraordinarily large number of 'baby boomers,' who will be drawing retirement incomes over the next thirty years, I believe it is reasonable and fair to levy a thirty year 3 percent surtax on annual incomes over one million dollars to increase revenues directed to the trust.

Should our legislature change our tax code to a non-progressive flat tax, then I believe the payroll tax should be replaced with a flat tax. Employers would match earnings to our current threshold, but the ceiling would be removed on employee contributions, resulting in a 6.2 percent payroll tax on all income; in which case a new income formula should be devised for income distribution based solely on the number of years worked rather than on the dollar amount contributed.

The current age for full retirement eligibility for a worker should be progressively raised from 67, the current age for one born in 1960 or later, to 70. Instead of the plan proposed by the Business Roundtable that substantially affects those under the age of 55, I propose a far more moderate approach. One additional month should be added to a workers retirement age from year 55 down. For example, a 55 year old would retire one month later than expected, a 54 year old, two months later, and a 19 year old, three years later, at age 70. This increase over a 36 year period is incremental, less punitive, and much fairer, for it allows adequate time to prepare for retirement.

Workers who have obtained 40 quarters of credit should remain eligible for partial Social Security withdrawal at age 62. A formula must be devised to determine the portion that will be received at age 62 based on income earned, employer contribution, age, and the number of years worked.

Currently, a non-working surviving spouse receives 71 percent of the working spouse's death benefit at age 60, and 100 percent at full retirement age. I believe that the surviving spouse should receive 100 percent of this accrued benefit at the time of the working spouse's death regardless of age.

No changes to Social Security eligibility should be made unless future funding is secured in an irrevocable guarded trust earmarked solely for the preservation of funds for their intended purpose.

CHAPTER THREE

MEDICARE, MEDICAID, AND
UNIVERSAL HEALTH INSURANCE REFORM

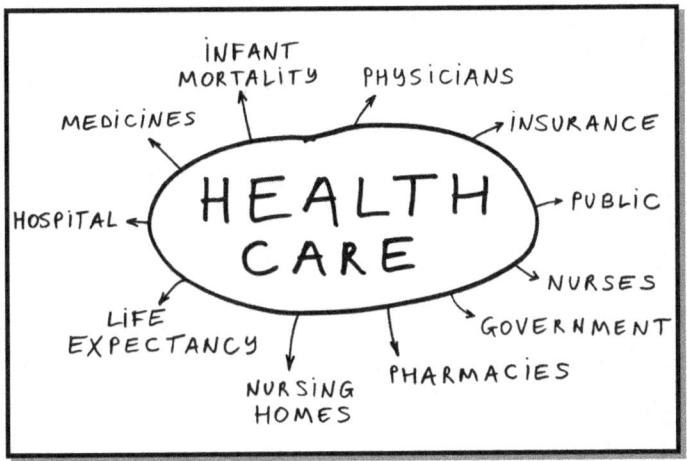

In 1975, healthcare expenditures accounted for 8.4 percent of America's GNP. Thirty-five years later, in 2010, at an average cost of $8,233.00 per person, healthcare costs were 17.9 percent of our GNP, nearly 2.5 times that of all other developed nations of the world. If action is not taken to drastically reduce this trend, by the year 2020, this percentage could very well approach 25 percent of the value of all goods and services produced in our country.

Spiraling healthcare costs are the concern of every American, because they are detrimental to the individual who has less disposable income to purchase goods and services and to invest in education and savings. They are damaging to businesses which contribute to employer sponsored health plans or suffer reductions in productivity as a result of illness related absenteeism incurred by those not covered. And, it is harmful to taxpayer-funded government budgets, which fund employee health plans and pay the healthcare costs of those on Medicare and Medicaid. Without realistic healthcare reform, these mounting costs will continue to be a drag on the economy, reduce our economic competitiveness, and divert money from other crucial programs in dire need of funding.

Congress should act immediately to streamline healthcare costs by combining programs, judiciously reducing fraud, and implementing major reforms. Sadly, it is highly unlikely that our representatives will implement modifications that will be in their constituent's best interests, because Congressional obstructionists are far more focused on the interests of lobbyists and their employers, and their own financial well-being, than the interests and the health of those they were elected to protect and serve.

To fully understand why our insurance system is so costly and why most forms of insurance are inflated, one must go back to the second half of the Twentieth Century when several of our largest insurance companies were mutual companies, and their primary obligation was to the insured. When these companies converted to stock companies, which provided windfall profits to top executives, their primary obligation shifted to the stockholder, thus adding an additional layer of costs to be paid in the form of dividends. Around the same time, managed care corporations began to emerge. Expected to substantially lower costs, they instead shifted payment from caregivers to administrators, capital improvements, and stockholders, thus adding additional layers of unnecessary outlays. To these layers of unnecessary distributions, we must add the billions spent on multiple insurance forms, and the hundreds of billions lost to fraud, unnecessary procedures, unwarranted administrative costs, and unjustified hospital admissions. It is estimated that these five alone may account for nearly 30 percent of all healthcare expenditures. We have transformed healthcare from an altruistic service to a greedy profit driven industry. And, in doing so, we have created a windfall for the insurance, managed care, and pharmaceutical companies, while squeezing profit margins for physicians and caregivers who have spent hundreds of thousands of dollars on education, while delaying, for nearly a decade, their entrance into the workforce. As for the insured, we have created insurmountable premium and patient-care cost burdens.

As part of Lyndon Johnson's 'Great Society" in 1965, Social Security Amendments resulted in the creation of two health programs: Medicare for the elderly and Medicaid for the poor. Under President Obama in 2011, a universal health plan was passed. Many in Congress opposed passage of our new universal care program, commonly referred to as 'Obamacare' because they consider it unaffordable, an intrusion into the private domain, and a prescription for disaster. However, these same veteran members of Congress failed to see a real 'prescription for disaster' when they allowed drug companies to formulate our current "Part D" Medicare drug program with no safeguard for the government to have the ability to negotiate for competitive pricing.

To summarize our present dilemma, healthcare costs are crippling our economy, and our representatives have not only done nothing to strengthen the two programs under our healthcare umbrella, but have further compromised their integrity by adding a third option to further weaken the system. Although credit must be given to President Obama for addressing the need and getting a universal plan in place, the plan, although comprehensive, is awkward, cumbersome, and unnecessary.

Before I recommend suggestions to improve healthcare, I want the reader to understand that I am a proponent of free enterprise and sincerely believe that capitalism is the best path to prosperity. That being said, I do not agree with unfettered capitalism, and I believe that there are several social programs such as Social Security, Medicare, and Medicaid that should be non-profit for they benefit Americans and, if refined and managed correctly, benefit our great nation.

My recommended healthcare reforms are quite simple. Combine our three current forms of government healthcare assistance into one single-payer, economically sound, cost effective, universal plan that covers all Americans, uses one standard form, adequately addresses fraud, rewards those who make lifestyle changes that enhance their health, and reduces unnecessary expenditures. This well-constructed plan must be designed to substantially reduce overall expenditures, increase doctor participation, address patient needs, and provide equitable payment to the actual providers of care, rather than to administrators and stockholders.

Instead of increasing payments to physicians, our current system continually reduces fees paid to Medicare and Medicaid providers, which discourages physicians from participating in these programs. In many cases, these substandard payments drive physicians from their chosen profession, which may likely lead to massive shortages of American doctors, who will be replaced by physicians from foreign countries. Therefore, the plan must contain provisions for educational subsidies that establish safeguards that prevent physician shortages from occurring as experienced by countries with comparable plans.

To understand why Americans should have one universal plan we need only to consider Medicare's prescription "Part D" coverage. Each insurer has a different plan, different costs, and different drug coverages. This program would be far more cost effective if every insurer was required to offer the same plan, price structure, and coverage, with government negotiation of competitive drug pricing. The "Part D" debacle illustrates that profit-driven multiple healthcare options, are confusing, unfair, and not cost effective.

Unreasonable medical costs have made it nearly impossible for all Americans to pursue our constitutionally guaranteed rights to 'life, liberty, and the pursuit of happiness" because we are often unable to seek adequate treatment, face economic ruin due to catastrophic illness, or forced to choose between nourishment and life sustaining prescription medications.

In the past, America rightly provided a safety health net to protect our aging population. We failed to provide the same for our youth, who will be our new wave of workers, and leaders who will determine the future of our great nation, and for the middle aged men and women who provide and consume the majority of goods and services that drive our economy. Surely the quality of healthcare provided to one generation should be available to all, especially when younger generations have fewer chronic illnesses and diseases and, therefore can subsidize and lower the overall costs of a universal program. If Medicare is a sound healthcare system for aging Americans, then it should be made accessible to all Americans.

The Senate attempted to lower Medicare eligibility to 55 in 2009, but was opposed by Senator Lieberman from the great insurance state of Connecticut. If this bill had passed, it might have opened the door for Medicare enrollment to all Americans.

It is not too late to incorporate 'Obamacare' and Medicaid into Medicare with premium assistance to eligible individuals and families. All Americans would be required to participate and would be covered regardless of pre-existing conditions, and all medical providers would be required to accept assignment. The result would be a single-payer system that could be streamlined and made far more efficient, far less fraudulent, much more effective, much simpler, and unequivocally less costly. I believe it is possible to reduce healthcare costs by 45-50 percent under such a system.

Of course the private business sector is not about to let 80 percent of healthcare revert to a non-profit single-payer system without a fight. Insurers would have to succumb to the realization they would receive only a portion of the pie by being limited to providing supplemental and prescriptive insurance, which would still give them 100 percent of both markets. And HMOs and PPOs could be prosperous if their business models were converted from reducing medical costs, to becoming the overseers of fraudulent activity, receiving a percentage of all deceptive activity. It is estimated that there is over 80 billion annually in Medicare fraud. If Medicare insures approximately 15 percent of our population, overall fraud in a one-payer system could potentially exceed 500 billion dollars annually in an expanded program, thus providing a function and revenue source for the managed care industry.

Americans should endorse and embrace such a concept, for we are a nation that believes in equality, and because we share one common inevitable fate: we age. It is rational to have one universal system to provide care continuity by covering every American through this aging process. Group insurance coverage through work is normally cheaper because it spreads risk across age brackets. Such a streamlined national Medicare group policy would do the same, but with far lower costs per person.

Younger generations may find this unfair and balk, because they have fewer chronic ailments. They must realize they too will age and incur many of the same ailments as our retirees. When they do, they will look toward subsequent generations for support. The majority of America's city and town tax revenues are earmarked for public education. Taxpayers support this allocation because they realize it is the civic responsibility of every American to ensure the next generation is well educated and able to become contributing members of society. It is fair to ask the youngest wage earners to support universal healthcare because our aging generations continue to support education funding through property taxes in the communities in which they live long after their children have since left the 'nest.' If seniors can pay for the education of the generations to follow, the largest budgeted expenditure for most American communities, why is it not the responsibility of younger generations to help subsidize the costs of the aging generation? If this is not a mutually agreeable arrangement for subsequent generations, perhaps the property taxes of couples without children and those whose children have completed public education should be directed to subsidize their healthcare rather than education.

To further substantially reduce premium costs for most Americans, our efforts to make lifestyle changes should be rewarded. Premium credits should be given to Americans who do not use recreational drugs, are not addicted to alcohol, are non-smokers, and are not chronically obese, because the top 5 percent of the population with chronic conditions account for nearly 50 percent of all health related expenses. And, all schools should become pro-active in the effort to eliminate obesity by introducing health classes into their curriculum, expanding existing gym classes to include more cardiovascular activity, and introducing after school intramural sport programs for those students not involved in competitive interscholastic sport.

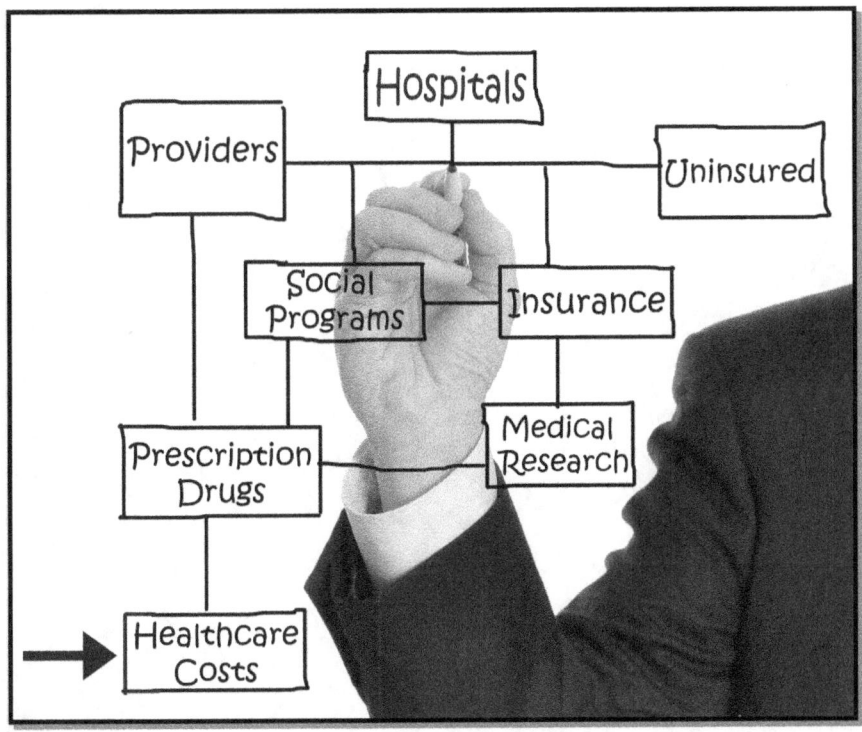

Every American should want our general population to be healthy, and every business should want their present and future workforce to be fit, for a healthy worker is generally a happy worker, and therefore, far more likely to be a productive worker. By pooling and simplifying healthcare coverage and lowering expenses, we will reduce premium costs for every American regardless of age, and in doing so, reduce expenditures for both the private and public sectors of our economy. A single-payer system will increase our nation's competitiveness; enhance our chances of eliminating deficits; reduce our country's debt; and minimize the future risks of hyper-inflation and rapidly accelerating interest rates.

CHAPTER IV

IMMIGRATION REFORM

There is no doubt that our immigration policy has been a complete disaster. It is estimated that over the last several decades, between 7 and 20 million immigrants have entered our country illegally, although 10 million is the most widely accepted estimate. Ironically, several of the most vocal among us, who express utter contempt for their presence and wish to immediately expel undocumented individuals from our shores, are often the same ones who looked away when immigrants crossed our borders, because they were in need of their services. Neither political party can escape blame as well, for members among both parties sought to either enhance their electoral base, or reap the benefits of cheap labor.

It is ludicrous and unjust to think that we can expel over 10 million inhabitants, most of whom have families and deep roots within society. Nor can we continue to ignore the fact that at least 10 million people have broken the law that has, for centuries, been followed by immigrants who also sought opportunity and refuge in our great nation, but selected the legal path to citizenship. Our immigration laws were constructed to allow an orderly entry into America, which included preventing criminals from entering our borders and the means and time for immigrants to learn our language, history, and culture and to assimilate into society. Many believe this massive circumvention of law has strained our judicial and penal systems, has deprived the government of billions of dollars in payroll and income taxes, has strained our healthcare system, and has dire economic and social ramifications yet to be fully realized. Americans are divided on the subject. Some want all immigrants to follow the prescribed course to citizenship, while others believe violators should be deported to their native lands. But, there is a growing number of Americans who believe that immigration reform is required to properly address the non-citizen issue in order to expeditiously direct undocumented individuals toward a simpler, less intimidating path to citizenship, which will allow their wholehearted assimilation into our general population. Before this can occur, most Americans agree that in order to prevent such a mass influx from occurring in the future, government must secure our borders and strictly control migration from foreign lands.

Before I address the issue of immigration reform, I wish to direct attention to a few of the facts and myths pertaining to undocumented immigrants living within our borders. Many Americans believe that those who have entered our country illegally pay no taxes. This is incorrect for a vast majority pay consumer taxes such as sales taxes and property taxes, and between 50-60 percent have payroll taxes deducted from their pay checks. Collectively, undocumented immigrants have contributed over 7 billion to Social Security, even though they are not eligible to collect benefits It is a general misconception that the majority of undocumented immigrants cannot speak English, for 67 percent speak our language fluently. It is also a mistaken belief that those who have entered our country illegally make up the greatest percent of incarcerated criminals, because according to the National Institute of Corrections, our citizens' make up the greatest percent of our prison population. Most Americans believe that nearly all undocumented immigrants are of Mexican heritage. Although they represent the fastest growing segment in our population, only 57 percent of undocumented immigrants are of Mexican heritage.

During prosperous times, migration from foreign lands is driven by employer demand as people follow the jobs and travel to America, the "land of opportunity." While economic expansion attracts, periods of economic contraction can slow immigration. It is not unusual to see migrations from specific geographic areas such as those which occurred from Europe during the 19th Century, or from particular countries like Ireland after the "Great Potato Famine" of 1845, when a potato blight destroyed their staple food crop, from China during 1865-1869 to work on our Transcontinental Railroad, and from South Vietnam and Cuba during the last half of the 20th century to escape communist rule and persecution. Because of our shared boundary, America's previous housing boom, split families living on opposite sides of the border, deplorable living conditions, and drug cartel violence, it is not difficult to understand why such a massive migration from Mexico took place during the latter part of the 20th century and first decade of the 21st century.

I am not condoning illegal entry, but rather trying to explain the aberration that occurred, especially from 2000-2005 when 8 million people migrated to America, 3.7 million of whom entered illegally, a number far greater than during any 5 year period of time in our history. Although the vast majority of undocumented entrees were from Mexico, large percentages were from Brazil and India.

The United States has been accused, by some nations, of being prejudicial and anti-immigration, which is ironic since America was colonized by immigrants, and in 2006 alone, America accepted more legal immigrants than the remaining countries of the world combined. The problems that most Americans have with massive, unrestricted, illegal migrations are real and understandable. Such unplanned influxes lead to concentration of settlements, which burdens our schools and educational budgets, strains community resources and infrastructures, and taxes emergency care centers. It also disrupts our voting processes, and poses serious concerns pertaining to social behavior and crime.

What must be done to reform illegal immigration is fivefold. First, we must take control of our borders. If we cannot screen and restrict who enters our country, then there is no need to further address the problem, because illegal immigration will remain a rampant, unmanageable problem. Second, we must address the path to citizenship for those living within our borders. If undocumented immigrants fear disclosure, they will remain in the shadows, continuing to derive income from unrecorded sources, while failing to properly integrate into society. Third, we must do thorough background checks and expel those who have felonious criminal records. Fourth, we must economically punish employers who hire undocumented workers. And fifth, we must levy sanctions against countries that attempt to deport felonious citizens to our shores, refuse to abide by our laws of immigration, and fail to readily support our deportation of those who either entered our country illegally or have committed violent crimes while awaiting the granting of U.S. citizenship.

It is estimated that the nautical coastline of America's 50 states is 12,383 miles. The combined land borders with Mexico and Canada, excluding Alaska, is approximately 3,471 miles, for a total border length of 15,854 miles. The number of U.S. border agents is 21,441, or roughly 1 per 2.2 miles per shift if evenly distributed. But, eighty-six percent of the total force is located on our southern border, leaving 3002 agents to cover 13,921 miles, or one agent per 13.9 miles if evenly distributed per shift. In a post 9/11 age when our country endures immigration surge and escalating terrorism at home and from abroad, it is obvious that additional manpower is needed to curb unlawful immigration and reduce the threat of a terrorist attack. Our country has withdrawn from Iraq and is in the process of withdrawing from Afghanistan. In 2012, the unemployment rate for returning troops departing from active duty was approximately 13 percent. Many of these veterans are deactivated national guardsmen who could be offered border patrol positions, which would firm up security, dramatically reduce illegitimate immigration, and lower unemployment.

By executive action, President Obama recently put in place a stop-gap measure which allows illegal immigrants under the age of 30, who have no criminal records, came to this country before the age of 16, are students, or have completed high school, or are vets in good standing, to remain in the country. This is a start, but does not address the remaining members of the families who wish to stay, but live in fear of deportation.

To fulfill citizenship requirements, our President and Congress must devise a fast-track method to facilitate and expedite the naturalization process so families can live without fear, and qualified applicants can be properly integrated into our society with an understanding of our culture and history, and a mastering of our language. Comprehensive integration will eliminate the shadow economy that circumvents fair wages and minimizes the chances of securing a decent standard of living and a higher level of education, prerequisites for a human being to develop a sense of security, an enhancement in social standing, and the development of a sense of national pride, requirements for a person to be a productive member of society. In the long term, proper integration will reduce the need for Medicaid and increase contributions to our tax base, and to our Social Security, Medicare, and universal health care systems. It will also permit those who have paid payroll taxes to qualify for benefits such as Medicare and Social Security as long as they can prove that they have filed and paid income tax on all prior earnings. It should also include a provision to allow those who have not done so to be given the opportunity to pay back-taxes on unreported income. And, it should provide a provision for allowing the elderly and those with dementia, Alzheimer's disease, and other severe learning disabilities to be exempt from restrictive language mastering requirements.

We cannot allow those who have entered our country legally to be by-passed for following the accepted path. Legal and undocumented immigrants without a criminal record should be required, within a three month period, to petition the Federal Government for a Pending Naturalization Certificate. If the background check is clear of felonious conviction here and abroad, a certificate will be issued. Failure to file a petition or disclose a felony conviction will result in the immediate removal of the applicant from our academic systems and from any local, state, and federal assistance programs. Vehicle and professional licenses will be nullified, and proceedings will be expedited to deport felons and non-participating, undocumented immigrants from our borders. Any applicant who is convicted of a felony during the naturalization process will also face immediate deportation.

Applicants who participate in this program will be allowed to remain in school and in any government assistance program in which they are currently enrolled. Under this program, all immigrants will be allowed to seek employment and apply for vehicle and professional licenses, and will be eligible for accelerated citizenship, a one time exception to naturalize those who desire to make America their home.

Unlike the Immigration Reform Bill of 1986 when Congress stripped many of the strong sanctions against employers who hired undocumented immigrants, this legislation must fully address the issue of employment. Employers should be granted three months to check and verify documentation of workers, but will be permitted to hire and keep immigrants who show they have petitioned and been accepted for this accelerated path to naturalization. Employers will receive a one time tax credit based on the number of employees to offset administrative costs incurred during this period of verification. Any employer who cannot show valid documentation after three months will be fined $25,000 for each invalid worker for the first fine, and $50,000 per worker thereafter. The one exception to this rule will apply to hiring talent from abroad in highly technical areas with proven shortages of qualified applicants. Provisional work permits will be granted to employees as long as these workers abide by our laws and receive pay equal to that of their American counterparts.

Applicants failing to gain citizenship through this fast-tracked program will be deported and will not be issued another Pending Naturalization Certificate. Individuals who immigrate from this date forward will not be eligible for a Pending Certificate or the augmented program.

It is not unprecedented to either grant amnesty or invoke exceptions to our Immigration policy. In 1986 President Reagan introduced the Immigration Reform Bill that granted amnesty to 3 million illegal immigrants who entered America before 1982. In the latter half of the 20th century, put in harm's way by our nation's political actions, Vietnamese and Cuban immigrants escaping Communist rule and persecution fled to our shores and were rightfully granted refugee status and asylum.

In a 1984 debate with Senator Mondale, President Reagan said of illegal immigrants living within the United States, "I believe in the idea of amnesty for those who have put down roots and lived here, even though sometime back they may have entered illegally."

Although the current number of undocumented people living

within our borders is estimated to be at least four times the number in 1984 and their conditions for migration different, the issue is the same. However, it is highly unlikely that Congress will approve an unqualified amnesty, for it alone will not rectify the complex problems associated with naturalizing and integrating 10 million plus immigrants into a population of over 300 million people, which is precisely why the need exists to reform the process.

Bill Clinton said, "America has constantly drawn strength from wave after wave of immigrants. They have proven to be the most restless, the most adventurous, the most innovative, and the most industrious." Yes, time has come to introduce meaningful and enforceable immigration reforms that will prevent mass incursions across our borders, deport non-naturalized criminals from our shores, and discourage undesirable migrants from entering our country. But, equally important is the need to formulate a policy that will encourage and allow those who have toiled our land and worked in our factories, raised families and developed deep roots within their communities, enhanced their education and social standing and have a burning desire to make America their acknowledged home, to come forth from the shadows with no fear of reprisal. In doing so, we unify our people, strengthen our economy, and show the nations of the world that the United States continues to be a beacon to those who possess the commendable qualities that have made our country an admired and enviable nation.

SUMMARY

America is the greatest nation, but we have temporarily lost our way, for we have strayed from the inherent qualities that have made us the envy of most other countries. We lack empathy for our fellow man, civility in our actions, restraint from entering conflict, and the will and resourcefulness to solve complex problems through negotiation. In addition, our complacency, lack of self-discipline, inability to compromise, and propensity for greed have decimated our economy and tainted our image as the indisputable guiding light of democracy and capitalism. We must correct our present course by reorganizing our priorities, restraining the arbitrary use of our military might, and exercising prudent monetary and fiscal policy.

It is often said that healthcare providers must care for themselves first, or they will be of little use to those who look to them for assistance. The same can be said of America in regard to our allies. No longer can we direct resources to other nations while depriving

Americans at home. No longer can we continue to place our forces in harm's way to defend regimes that do not desire or warrant our assistance, or dishonor and threaten our people. And no longer can we place the welfare of other nations ahead of our own.

America's greatest immediate threat is our national debt, which continues to mount and is rapidly approaching a sum that will soon make it impossible for future revenues to service the indebtedness which threatens our nation's sovereignty. We recently avoided an economic meltdown because depressed economic conditions allowed the FED to artificially hold interest rates at historically low levels, and because our recent recession coincided with the end of a 26 year downward interest rate cycle. However, if nothing is done to increase revenues and reduce our liabilities and a new upward interest rate cycle were to begin and rates were to reach their modern historical average of 6.9 percent, America would surely be on the brink of economic Armageddon. If rates were to ever approach the double digit rates of the '70s that saw prime rates peak at 21.5 percent, our economy would collapse, and along with it, the economies of most of the world. Considering the seriousness of our situation and the consequences that a potential United States default could one day trigger, Congress should be far more concerned with passing reforms that will prevent such a catastrophic event from happening; modifications constructed to raise revenues and reduce expenditures, eliminate annual deficits, and reduce our spiraling national debt. If our legislative branch passes reforms that are fair and productive and are in the best interests of all Americans and not the special interests that currently have undue influence on Congress, Americans will be far more supportive of changes that require sacrifice.

It is possible Congress chooses not to formulate constructive legislation because they hope to avoid blame should their decisions lead to a further destabilization of markets and a continued disintegration of public confidence, although this is hard to believe considering the low esteem we currently have for our elected representation. It is conceivable that close affiliations with lobbyists have provided our representatives with a false sense of security that allows them to believe their economic welfare is cushioned from such a cataclysmic economic implosion. We know a substantial number are more concerned with party-lines than in bi-partisan cooperation. Perhaps, as in the past, they think default could never happen if they remain deadlocked and do nothing. But, if the latter is the most likely cause, they need only to look to debt-ridden Southern Europe; to Greece, Portugal, Spain, Ireland, and Italy, or to the city of Detroit, which is only one of many American cities facing bankruptcy, since a good number appear unable to continue to service their debt. It is my belief we simply overestimate our representatives' ability to solve problems, because most members of Congress are politicians rather than 'statesmen' and are simply incompetent and incapable of developing and negotiating rational solutions to complex problems. Whatever the reasons, Congress has avoided compromise and prevented rational and fiscally prudent legislation from being passed, making most members appear unworthy of the offices to which they were elected.

Our indebtedness is not our only concern. We face growing threats from abroad from Iran and North Korea, and from radical Islamic terror groups like Al Qaeda, which threatens the safety of our people and our allies, and have added trillions of dollars to our debt. And, we are hesitant to address the inappropriate conduct of one of our largest trading partners and holders of US debt, because we do not wish to offend China, a country that one day may become our greatest military adversary.

Our dangers are not solely from abroad. We are a polarized nation, politically divided on immigration and wealth distribution, on healthcare and entitlements, and between those who favor an omnipotent Federal government and those who prefer greater state control. Centuries of mistrust and resentment may one day again erupt in civil conflict if our representatives are unable to work together to re-balance power and resolve conflicts in a way that will pacify our two major parties and unify our great nation. States must realize that a population of over 300 million requires a strong federal government to defend our people, deal with catastrophic climatic events, and care for our sick, poor, and elderly. The Federal Government must recognize that there is a Constitutionally mandated balance of power which delegates authority to states to self-govern, and that they must to do so within the limitations of a balanced budget.

Dysfunctional government is not our only internal concern, for government alone cannot address and rectify our growing debt. The public and private sectors of our economy must work in harmony because each is dependent on the other as our economy periodically transitions between expansions and contractions. But extreme, immoral behavior by either sector is no longer acceptable. Rampant spending must be reined in and unfettered capitalism disallowed. The public and private sectors must work together to create jobs that give workers and their families the money required to purchase goods and services, for demand is the machine that drives the economy, although supply-side economists would like you to believe differently. Driven partially by greed and the lack of clear direction from government, banks and big corporations are hoarding more cash than during any time in history. In order for this money to be reinvested in the economy, it is imperative that Congress provide the leadership and clarity required to maintain fiscal discipline and encourage growth.

America is slowly coming to grips with the economic consequences of unfunded spending on two wars and a massive tax cut. But, if we fail to care for our sick, poor, and elderly who are truly incapable of caring for themselves, we will increase civil anxiety. If we do not reduce our debt to enable us to honor the entitlements to which hard working Americans contributed and expect compensation, we will have civil unrest. And, if we don't reduce the great disparity between the ultra rich and the remaining population, we will have civil war.

In 2009, the top 400 people in America had amassed $1.27 trillion in wealth, while the bottom 50 percent had less than 1.22 trillion in assets. Less than 1 percent of the wealthiest Americans have amassed more wealth than the bottom 50 percent of our general population. It is estimated that by 2050, the sum of our current minorities will become the majority. If this does occur, our greatest threat will be from within, because such wealth disparity in prior great civilizations has resulted in a total restructuring of governments.

Revenues alone will not mend the economy, firm markets, and address our indebtedness. To rid ourselves of debt, we must reduce obscene asset inequality and modernize entitlements to honor past commitments and ensure their continuance. An immediate collective effort must be made to reform our tax code, Social Security, Medicare, Medicaid, Universal Healthcare, and Immigration programs. Reforms must be incrementally implemented that reduce entitlement spending, which has doubled since the 1960s, in a manner that honors prior commitments made to those who have funded these programs for years with the promise of future redemption. The amendments should be rear-loaded, which will not stall our recovery, but will have long term ramifications that will guide us on a path to prosperity.

President Obama and Congress must decide if they want to modify our existing progressive tax code or revert to a flat tax. If they favor our current code, which is overly complicated, cumbersome, and fosters "irrational individual behavior and corporate avoidance," then unfair and irrational loopholes that solely favor the rich and special interests must be abolished. Should a flat tax be considered the fairest method, all taxpayers must be treated equally by having one standard deduction of $50,000 regardless of personal circumstances. Congress should not give consideration to a European-style sales tax that penalizes goods and services at every stage of production and dramatically impacts the least affluent.

Most post WWII 'Baby Boomers' who began working in the early 1960s began receiving Social Security checks in 2008. We as a nation, have a moral obligation to guarantee these checks will continue. Misuse of funds, an expansion in life expectancy, and spousal withdrawals have destabilized the integrity of the fund. To guarantee future benefits, one month should be added to a worker and spouse's retirement age from 55 downward so that a 19 year old entering the workforce will qualify for full retirement at age 70. All retirees must accumulate 40 quarters of payroll contributions to qualify for retirement income. Those who have not qualified under their own merit, but wish to receive retirement income should be required to have their working spouse contribute an additional 50 percent of their payroll contribution for each missing quarter to reach the required quarter limit. Surviving spouses, regardless of age, should immediately qualify for death benefit income at the time of the working spouse's death. Workers with incomes exceeding one million dollars should be subject to a 3 percent payroll surtax.

Healthcare expenditures account for nearly 17 percent of our current GNP and must be curtailed, because they are damaging to consumers, to businesses, and to local, state, and the Federal Government which funds employee healthcare programs. They are a drag on our economy, reduce our economic competitiveness, and divert monies from other crucial programs in need of funding. Congress should act immediately to streamline costs by combining Medicaid and 'Obamacare' with Medicare, establishing a single-payer, cost-effective, efficient system that will reduce fraud and deceptive practices and eliminate unnecessary procedures and hospital emissions. The new Universal system must reward individuals who make healthy lifestyle changes and schools that add health classes, increase cardiovascular activity in gym classes, and introduce after-school intramural sport programs. By pooling and simplifying healthcare, standardizing costs and placing it under the jurisdiction of one administration, it will lower expenses, substantially reduce premiums, and increase compensation to physicians and healthcare workers who actually provide a medical-related service.

There is little doubt that our immigration procedures have been a disaster. But, it is ridiculous to think that we can expel over 10 million undocumented inhabitants, many of whom have deep roots within society. Nor can we allow future unrestricted mass migrations to our borders, for such massive influxes burden our schools and education budgets, strain community resources and infrastructures, tax emergency care centers, disrupt voting processes, and pose serious concerns pertaining to social behavior and crime. We must take control of our borders and address the path to naturalization for all who await, or wish to seek citizenship. And, we must expel those with felonious records, punish employers who hire undocumented workers, and levy sanctions against countries that refuse to abide by our laws of immigration or fail to readily accept those we deport back to their native lands.

Reforms are not the only matters that need to be addressed to strengthen our economy and ensure our sovereignty. Globalization and outsourcing have taken most manufacturing and a good number of service jobs overseas. Currently, companies are slowly beginning to return to our shores, because shipping and labor costs abroad are beginning to rise, while labor costs at home have remained stagnant. But many of these jobs have been replaced with robots or other forms of automation. Some say we need a new paradigm to boost our economy. This may be true, but in the meantime the one area that doesn't require robotics and should never be outsourced is internal investment. Since the 1960s, government investments in infrastructure are down 50 percent. It is estimated that by the year

2020, America will experience a 40 percent shortfall in infrastructure spending. We can increase employment and strengthen our economy by fully developing both our exhaustible and renewable sources of energy, by investing in technologies that enable us to better allocate natural resources including our precious water and energy supplies, by improving the quality of education, and by repairing, expanding, and modernizing our schools, roads, dams, bridges, high-rises, and power grids. And we can continue to modernize our military forces to prepare for the day when future superpowers may test our resolve.

Thomas Jefferson said, "It is incumbent on every generation to pay its own debt as it goes." Our country's leadership has continually failed to heed the advice of one of our greatest Founding Fathers. It is time we address our liabilities for we have mortgaged the future of countless generations to follow and jeopardized the future sovereignty of our great nation.

Jefferson also said, "The greatest good we can do our country is to heal its party divisions and make them one people." It is not too late to heed these words as well and put our country's welfare ahead of party-lines. However, time is running out. As FED Chairman Ben Bernanke told Congress, "The best time to start addressing the problem was 10 years ago. There is still time to fix it. But ignoring the problem-just like hanging up on the debt collector-is not a great thing to do." Let us not ignore our debt collector, for we will not be prepared for the economic and political consequences that follow.

ABOUT THE AUTHOR

Author Roy Eaton is a graduate of New York Military Academy, where he served as a cadet captain. Roy earned a Bachelor of Science Degree from Pennsylvania Military College where, as a senior, he became the only student in the college's history to be elected student government president, senior class president, and brigade honor court president. He also received the army's Distinguished Military Student Award, and was a member of the Pershing Rifle National Champion Drill Team, the cadet brigade staff, and the varsity wrestling team.

Roy Eaton earned a Masters Degree from Connecticut College, and a commission in the U.S. Army Reserve Officers Corps. Roy taught mathematics and wrestling at St. Bernard High School in Uncasville, Connecticut, and was the first faculty member elected to the school's Board of Trustees. He has been included in the publications "Who's Who Among Students in America, and "Who's Who Among America's Teachers."

At the age of 26, Roy Eaton was elected the Connecticut's first team coach by the Connecticut Freestyle Wrestling Federation. Although Roy started the Saints wrestling program and coached for only seven years, his former high school teams have been cited by the town of Montville, Connecticut, and the state's Legislature and Governor for their outstanding performance. Nine of his former wrestlers became high school head wrestling coaches. Roy is a member of the St. Bernard Athletic Hall of Fame, the New York Military Academy Sport Hall of Fame, and the city of New London, Connecticut's Athletic Hall of Fame. In June of 2006, at the National Sports Achievement Dinner held on Marco Island, Florida, Eaton was awarded the lifetime achievement award in wrestling. In June of 2007, he delivered the commencement address at the New York Military Academy, and in 2009 Roy's lifetime achievements were recognized by his Hometown City of New London, and by the Connecticut State Legislature. Eaton's first book, the autobiography, *Soldier Boy*, was endorsed by Donald J. Trump and published in 2006. Roy's second book, *The Chosen Few*, was published in 2008, and his third book, *Makers, Shakers, and Takers*, was published in 2012. Roy will again deliver the commencement address at the New York Military Academy June 1, 2013.

www.ingramcontent.com/pod-product-compliance
Lightning Source LLC
Chambersburg PA
CBHW070623290526
45790CB00002B/961